THE BAD WIFE

MICHELINE MAYLOR

The Bad Wife

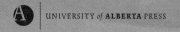

UNIVERSITY *of* **ALBERTA** PRESS

Published by

University of Alberta Press
1–16 Rutherford Library South
11204 89 Avenue NW
Edmonton, Alberta, Canada T6G 2J4
uap.ualberta.ca

LIBRARY AND ARCHIVES CANADA
CATALOGUING IN PUBLICATION

Title: The bad wife / Micheline Maylor.
Names: Maylor, Micheline, 1970– author.
Series: Robert Kroetsch series.
Description: Series statement: Robert Kroetsch
     series | Poems.
Identifiers: Canadiana (print) 20200406450 |
     Canadiana (ebook) 20200406507 |
     ISBN 9781772125481 (softcover) |
     ISBN 9781772125580 (PDF)
Subjects: LCSH: Marriage—Poetry.
Classification: LCC PS8626.A9328 B33 2021 |
     DDC C811/.6—dc23

First edition, first printing, 2021.
First printed and bound in Canada by Houghton
Boston Printers, Saskatoon, Saskatchewan.
Copyediting and proofreading by Alice Major.

A volume in the Robert Kroetsch Series.

University of Alberta Press is committed to
protecting our natural environment. As part of
our efforts, this book is printed on Enviro Paper:
it contains 100% post-consumer recycled fibres
and is acid- and chlorine-free.

University of Alberta Press gratefully
acknowledges the support received for its
publishing program from the Government of
Canada, the Canada Council for the Arts, and
the Government of Alberta through the Alberta
Media Fund.

Oh, I have made myself a tribe
out of my true affections,
and my tribe is scattered!
How shall the heart be reconciled
to its feast of losses?
—"The Layers," Stanley Kunitz

CONTENTS

HOW TO BECOME A BAD WIFE

Start with the archetype of innocence. Start as the lawful good, let the Kraken dice fall on good favour. Start with a long white sun-dress, strappy sandals, and bring a puppy. Flirt. Look wide-eyed at the world with brown swirling fingers. Point at dreams and purple mountain bluebells. Use brown sugar in your coffee. Sweeten everything. Once sure you are being followed by the man, let the tan of your ankle show. Hide the barnyards of your life in the hem of your skirt. Daub the light pink eyeshadow from Shoppers Drug Mart in the corner of your lids. Appear fresh. You must look good to make the effects really last before you turn dark.

Turn dark after the vows. Wait until after the first born and the second born. Secure your sweetness in their DNA. Then experience the rock-slide of your own heart, skiff across doubt's surface. Slide slowly, gather dirt and wounds. Stay calm and frightening, a temple guardian of the heart. Envision lizards running on water. Panic at your own life. Find yourself someone to talk to. A nice professor much older than you. Always safe. Go somewhere with coffee. Be sure the children are with the babysitter. Start sinking, not skimming. Become an unreliable narrator. Find danger as water invades your ears, sunlight loyal above you. See the patterns on the surface ripple and shake. Here is the diaphanous. Find yourself drowned. Utter your own epitaph from underneath the seas. Here lies. Here lies the bad wife.

EPITHALAMION:
THE GRAND CANYON WAS A LONG WAY DOWN

Because you were a pale-skinned Adonis
with your weed whipper and plaid shorts
mowing the lawn of your brown house,
I became new butter in coffee, drippy

and spilt on the shop table. You turned
a wrench and thunder bellowed. Me: stamen-
stung with flowers along the back 40
Marry me or I'll push you in, you asked.

That proposal! My mind was a wind-ripped
bumble-bee, a dieting chickadee stuffed
with tomorrow's sweet honey mead,
and the ring-stone was green.

Your voice was a leaping tourist,
and yes, there's a donkey for rent.

THE MEAN GAME

After J.W.B.

Even the collage wears Janus eyes,
a furrowed brow, a white-high forehead.
Their body is a two-person hour-glass
a teaming father/daughter twin,

a two-person war machine for whom
I will never be a neutral territory.
This is the stuff of Shakespearean tragedy.
Fools heft mud and brick into a gravesite,

my stone reads, *Happily Ever After, here lies*
mother, villain, squire of this tainted land.
From this earth spring all the poison flowers
born from her ribs and her breasts. Her bones seed

reasons for all earth's destruction, all
of the rising seas, all of the dying bees.

I bought the too tough, new cherries from Washington, packed organic meat, high-pink cupcakes. The sun, in the right place in the sky for remembering you, hot and wilting light slanted into the past. The salt-sweat pits, my arms drip heavy with fresh produce from Leduc. If this were a decade ago, I'd return to our porch, after having slid summer sausage into our freezer, and snap peas into the mouths of our children. I'd have had lime-soda while you changed the oil in your car in the back yard. I'd sigh summer's exhale. I'd have accounted for our neighbours, counted like suspects. Accounted for the known and familiar, named kids as they jumped rope and on trampolines. I'd expect you around with your four o'clock wine and grease-stained jeans to sit with me at the top of the verandah stairs as the grey squirrels and tabby cats ran hide and seek. "There's a face in the bark of that tree," our daughter says, "I don't know why, but I don't think he's happy." She already states her worldview a short phrase at a time. I give her a platitude in a plastic bag, ask her to recycle. I should have consulted the executives in the boardroom, asked for a redo. I forgot the oath: Do no harm.

THE CROW TAKES THE BODY

I take the body from the cold, wet, slate stones,
from under the eaves, from under the neck-break window,
from under the sill, from under the bushes and the wilted mint.
I take the body to the high grass, beside the small red bush,
long-branched in the long, long grass, wet beside wilting
wildflowers, offer up for the scavengers the beautiful body,
to magpie, to crow. The crow sees the body first, curls in,
glides a circle, an eye circle, a wind circle. The circle crow
takes the robin who dies by window, and on camera,
where I shoot last gulping breaths, contracting legs and heart,
I shoot them in my camera until two convulsions make
a death out of a life and I watch my camera witnessing
the last of this little mottled heart. And the body stays
on the slate, on the wet stone, until I offer her to the grass,
to the red brush, and crow comes, on time, the undertaker
arrives too late, and the crow takes the body into its beak,
and takes the weight, bows to the sky, gives thanks I think,
lifts into the near trees and fog, sits down solemn and bows
to the body, an offering from the window, and the grass,

and me.

I cut our sex life out of memory for the scrapbook. The results were mediocre. I prefer the corner where I collaged the green convertible onto the back-country road, on that September evening. I must have been drunk. I remember rummaging the glove box for a map or income taxes or an oracle. An ace of swords for cutting clean.

You disappear from my dreams one woken sun-flake at a time. I kill you with my forgetting. It's our best shot at taking each other for granted one last time.

Our daughter suggests that we try to get along. I have no quarrel with you or standing in the same room. It's complicated. Optimism and pessimism grumble, at odds with complacency. You don't return my texts. This sentence lacks imagery. I watch the weeds flare after the August rainstorm, little cheering fans at the rock concert with their cellphone flashlights glittering. The sky smudges puss grey. I wonder about the free will of clouds. How they shapeshift. Right out of their own selves before scudding off into oblivion.

YOUR MOTTO

I told you once I love you; if anything changes, I'll let you know.
—*attributed to* John Wayne

I couldn't stay faithful after New Year's Eve,
all those aggressive philosophy majors and tequila shots.
You and me sat, the stuffed bears in our son's room
propped up in corners, staring, neglected, a bit dusty.
What was to be done after that party? All my switches
flipped, a fuse box shutting down. Click by click.
Time to wrap it up, kids. Last call. Last song.
And I'm sitting here in my corner now, hearing you say,
"What'd you want me to do, punch the guy?"
No. No. No. I wanted you to love me so hard,
that he didn't have space to demand I go home with him.
I wanted you to love me, but you were too busy laughing.

THE SLEEP

In this radical edit, I walk out of an elegy carrying a haiku.
I look for a glimpse of my married life somewhere between REM and dawn.

I have no argument with you. This is irony.
The forever dream house renamed itself The Albatross.

Our children moan like bagpipes. Until they stop.
A dead winter rabbit silently stank up the spring lilacs.

Its rotten carcass upended on your shovel, then all of my things.
Even the locket on my bracelet needed to be re-keyed.

The neighbour said, *you're good together*. I disagreed.
The front porch drunks wanted a happy ending.

Honestly.
No one tells a good bedtime story anymore.

Ankles, the sexiest part of a woman, you said. That feminine dip and curve of that boney slip and jut before the arch of the foot swoops towards enticement. The bad wife takes to wearing short pants and kitten heels. The bad wife takes eyes down the school halls, gazes pinched between her fingers, hauled like naughty boys caught shooting spitballs. The bad wife takes the professor to the laundromat, washes his brain out with soap and sweet words. It's as if they've all stepped onto the streets of Paris for the first time. Everyone is in awe of all the good planning, the crossed lines. Such elegance. In the streets: fountains, the riverbank, the bakeries, the fresh market fish, dog-shit. The wrong shoes, a misstep, a joint torqued blue.

TWO MEN

> Two men can keep a secret if both of them are dead.
> —Ben Franklin or my dad

The bad wife thinks of details at odd times. Japanese bowls at Christmas.
The bad wife becomes a narrative among your good friends.
Accept the narrative. Say, cautionary. Say, not pretty.
You glue a collage: my portrait done in skin flakes and maggots.

The story is not footage I shot for public consumption.
One of us will be living somewhere else in six months. Sentimentally,
I kept a video of the love song with the roller-skating girls and the moose.
The lawyer accounted the socks from the Highland gift shop, divided by two.

A sock for me. A sock for you. The last time we made love, the hotel in Missouri.
Twice. Months after, nothing electric happened. Proof.
The last few dinners at a notable bar. You knew me too well.
I said, *I'm disappointed* and you said. Nothing. Then, *I am who I am.*

The oil price layoffs. The tension in your shoulders. Accumulated.
The last time you tried to touch me, I flinched. I think,
how to let go? Easy. Drop a snow globe. See for yourself.
I wonder what it is like to write this from the other side of our time and space.

There are so many ways to tell our friends of this hoax. Not a hoax.
From this far off we are the tiny people stiff, spilled. I did not want
to believe I had cheated. I want to apologise because ... But.
All at once, that sort of devastation is too much to bear.

Just keep doing what you're doing.

You're a natural.

(N)EVER THOUGHT

I've been having home-wreck dreams of you.
I've got an inside view from our big window.
This is a metaphor, of course, not a manufacture, yet.
We stay shrouded in a cloud of disaster.

Dust in the loader bucket, the ideal view ruins itself.
This dream is all I could pull out of the dark.
A toothy, wild punk drunk at the controls.
I get ornery when unprotected.

I'm the wife at the party guarded by friends'
husbands who have more vigilant shoulders.
Some big bully wants me for his own.
You have such lovely smiling dimples when you watch.

Over there in the corner, you eye the trespasser.
He drives right into your marriage and you watch.

I sought you out for your resemblance to a single moment I wrote in my diary in August of 1980. Inside information. I did not integrate my Jungian dark side and left a dangling, waving prayer flag in the wind, a subconscious rod for trouble and sexual deviancy. What is a life to do but deliver exactly what you want — that you don't know you wanted. Be careful what you ask for on a breeze.

I knew I would destroy you. What you don't know will kill you. Isn't that the motto of every fairy tale before the jaws of the fur-kin bite and blow out like a summer vacation of Hubba Bubba bubbles, delighted and laughing, but exploded just the same?

I knew my brown ankles would do the trick. I should have avoided the gravel alley where you stood. I should have hidden in the doom-oracle puddles that were shaped like the Lotus Cortinas my father used to fix in the garage before the north shore waves of despair broke on my fantasy of happy families. Was I so hard to hear? In the fall, I sit close to dogwood, dye my hair red with henna, to match these Mordor eyes.

We fly into Kansas for Maker's Mark and local draft.
The man in the bar plays Muddy Waters for silver,
for paper tips, for cattle drives. The shower is strong
hot and orgasmic. An organic restaurant blackens fish
near the antique place with buckets of doll heads,
old card catalogues turned into wine racks. Smoke spits
the sky as we drive into Missouri. Tiredness makes bones
crisp. The Georgian guest house gives oranges, fried eggs
for breakfast. We roam the King-sized bed with maroon
sheets. Glass rabbits watch and I wonder what to hold
in my palm. I cut my leg shaving. The nick bleeds. The sheets
say nothing to the landlord. We have the last-best sex.
On all fours, I thank the footboard. It's quite the operation
running that body of land, that Inn. We walk past the algae pond,
into red October-turned bushes. Autumn rolls in, a lamb, and sleeps
into winter, waiting for the slow-motion exit I start to make.
There is a picture of me in a grey jacket against a brick wall.
Above, the sky says nothing. It's almost all shade.

Cold golden under the halogen, the smooth soft bone looks nothing like the devil's bronze knuckle smoothing a slick, glossy vulva. Nor does a clavicle look like a lie. Although, a fibber's text could be written there across the nude line in invisible ink. A bad spell, a summoner's prayer, a white tattoo to read backwards in the mirror.

THE PINE SISKIN

Last week, I drew rebirth from my Druid deck
then came a small thunk at the front window
a small wreck, a little plunk. Snow still thick

in the garden, vanishing, spring's magic trick.
I drank of my warm coffee and cool silence.
Searching for something else, a life hack,

an inside yearning, a witchy tarot pack.
The siskin flew straight, an unnoticed fellow
delivering a gooey, esoteric message: *take*

a closer look, somewhere near the back
of your mind, the path you seek, leads—somehow—
to satisfaction, if you look. Optimistic and thick

in the head, I focused on the black rabbit,
the fucker, in the art of the card and mellow
light of the room, not the imminent smack

of a tiny life dropping to death, a fresh wreck
at my door. Today, the pine siskin stays fallow
in the yard, loosing feathers to the wind and rock
where I laid him, a meal for friends: raven and rook.

If anywhere, the silty sand and the raining ash marked the start of this apocalypse. I could not overcome my own existential smudge-year crisis. Forest fires tinted the sky sick grey-green-black, ash flakes fell, snow of a strange season. We tried. We took the children to the beach, swam as the water bombers scooped out bits of lake to douse the burning forest just over the pass, and we slept in the hollowed-out rented bed with something between us. Was it a child, or a dog, or a canyon? Details don't matter. We tried. The dusty-rose bedspread and the uneven sleeping porch used up all my bandwidth. Although, a specific image of you: kissing our daughter goodnight on her forehead in the cabin-stacked bunk beds. I imagine her relief, that safety you gave while the smoke came in the south-west windows, murked the sky black. Why did I feel it necessary to take my bag and run as if the vow said, every woman for herself?

THE CROW GIVES A BODY

Not good with divination or dandelion,
on an afternoon's seeking. I sneak to the monks'
cemetery, hoping the faithful-dead could speak,
Father Alphonse what can you tell
about the gory art of preservation?

A white moth stayed mum. There, an oracle
of robin's breast lay bombed out in grass, a life gone
sad, gone, speckled shrapnel in clover,
sly witness to this set of telling ruins,
an amateur's prophesy, an awkward spread.

A foreshadow of wealth, or a punch in the mouth
with a chalice. Something about love? *Nothing lasts.*

THE BAD WIFE'S VULVA

Fallow as a nature reserve lined with bamboo sticks and the Latin names
of fauna, rickety warnings to stay away from the habitat restoration area.
Tern eggs tucked in the verdant brush and slim ovary of the seawall. The bad
wife's vulva opens out, a rusty door, after an open sesame on Christmas and
birthdays, sometimes in the car under exciting fingers, sometimes after drinks,
after the shops, after a phlegmy cough, sometimes when the dog is watching.
Sometimes, not at all.

PORTRAIT OF MY LIFE AS A NURSE LOG

Ultraviolet petals feather off the flowering Jacaranda.
On the highway, we pass Road Trip Jesus and Paper Bag Buddha.
They wave from the backseat of a night-blue Nissan.

Two Gods gone to visit National Parks with marked trails, protected. Nice.
Prophets on the gravel road to green-green pristine.
An omen-wind's percussion bothers the red elephant fungus.

The rock chute from a volcano clears its nostrils of stone.
At the cemetery a rooster eats the mourning bouquet.
I'd like to believe my life is worthy of all this decay.

GUILT

I left her, the dog, when I bereaved my husband,
because I became a nomad. This is not an excuse.
It's an explanation for why ants have morphed
into red, miniature bull terriers on the garden path.

Because I am a nomad, this is now an excuse
for letting go, unclamping my unhinged life
while an unhinged bull terrier on the garden path
gnaws at a tiny bone from the Past Life Pet Shop.

Let go. Repeat the misunderstood. Unhinge a life
after a prize fight. Don't return to this ring.
Unleash the bull terrier on the garden path!
I left her, the dog, when I bereaved myself.

DIVORCE SUDOKU

columns of expenses	new shoes for daughter	gym credits for son
who pays the drums	sign off on support	layoffs and questions
working five jobs	who owes who what?	sometimes love
sparrow in the house	daughter buys a motorbike	a tattoo or two
son in the basement	video game night	out with a friend
home with the kids	friends have questions	party with pot
we blow each other off	sometimes	so many times
with questions	sometimes not	what should fit
misplaced	doesn't matter	start again

SO, SAY I

Say, I will, say I do, doo-be-doo-be-doo-be-doo. Say, seashell, and ambergris,
say wibble-bobble, say Chablis. Say, French-blue, say, skinamarinka-doo, I love
you. Say, verdigris, say university, say auburn, say wimple, say I am not a saint,
say dip-shit, say mistake, say I tried, say you gave up, say whatever you need
to move on, say excuse, say weariness, say something hard to swallow, say a
prayer to your atheist friend. Say Windex, never see clearly again. Say morning.
Say, take it back. Would I take it back? Say I take it back, would you take me
back? Say handshake, say lawyer, say sign right here on the flagged lines. Say
bedsheets, say ticking, say timebomb, say bourbon, say my name on the cusp
of a fiery swill, say swing-set, say tree-stump, say sunset. Say it like you mean it.
Oh, I meant it when I said it.

THE MORAL RESPONSIBILITY TO BE INTELLIGENT

Some dumbass like you
might be your ancestor?
It's probably true.

THIS IS MY 21ST WEDDING ANNIVERSARY

Cremate me with barbed wire and whip-crack tears in an oven of river rock draped with snake skins. Lavender seeds moult out of my tear ducts. Knowledge smears underneath sneaker treads, slippery and dank. Inventory of the years slips from my knowing, oily and peeled. I had a dram of your scotch on the deck of the ship where we hunted abyssal fish. Those toothy bastards grinned needles. Ferociously. Your hands gripped tight on their tails. How you tried your best to protect me from snapping jaws. You've turned mean in my dreams and tired. I so thoroughly wore you out. I clubbed you in the bucket. You wear your baseball hat to keep out the cold grey water, sharp on the skin. Wake and sorrow flecked on our cheeks. I don't know what to make out of all this remembering. If I dive in, will you recall that I loved you, somehow the ripples still do. Still do. Still do. Still.

Sometimes, I plunk an apple into the lake, toss wind-blown seeds.
Hurl a bone past the lip-licking fire into long grass and weeds.

A hungry mouth in the darkness, a gnashing tiny beak.
Whittling its bones, stomach to skin. Speak now, or forever...

Earth growls, a craving beast, and I'm rich with eats.
Pitch a little to the loam, the bacteria and fungi, at least.

Ants will make a meal out of the whole of me:
eyeballs, calluses, my throwaway ring-finger and teeth.

SHE TELLS ME

The toilet in the basement has belched up and over
its intestinal wreckage, drained-stained the floor
like a party goer drunked up and shaken sober.

In my new office, I've become the scapegoat
for my grandmother's guilt. I've become a beacon
of success. I hardly pick up the phone anymore.

She tells of irrelevant relatives, cinema
I walked away from. I tell her how you taught
the art of dehydration. I was so parched.

THERE IS NO WORD

For waking neighbours with noisy sex.
For the taste of wasabi.

For not hearing what I said.
For crotch split pants.

For fucking that other girl's boy.
For the stupidity of not seeing the doctor.

For a talent for fixing things.
For how slowly we move.

For wine in the afternoon.
For that mood when I call you and you're stoned.

For life's trembling, whacked-out complexity.

REASONS FOR MY HUSBAND'S INATTENTIVENESS

On a midweek day-drunk, full-frontal kidney massage,
the gale-force wind whispered into my temples,
You have a misery problem...
What delight when a day spells its truth!

Rollers break on the north shore, a salt lick tongued.
My organs are bagpipes, soft and moaning.
They won't talk back because the wind is right
for holding onto this pout, this disharmony. Tight.

STYX AND STONES

I have a secret wilderness I keep inside, tight as spider-eggs
tucked in for the winter and waiting to be far flung, strung,
then tamped tight as a forest floor. What visions turn to currency?

Now that anger is done, I've devastated you like a Wall Street
banker on a Saturday bender. We all have new traditions now.
Nothing looks like it used to. Get over it. Stuff in tight any remorse.

Hang long memories, cinch those unwanted puppies in the killing sack!
My shoes are milk-thistle kitten heels, almost remorseless and almost vast.

VAGABOND

Let me say, I have been accused of many things,
mercurial, caustic, hot-blooded. I've been a home wrecker,
witch, savior, mentor, mother. Let me say, I have been all
those things; I have read the Kama Sutra after midnight
in a rented house, until it ran in my blood.
I bent a lover like a whim and leached all the pleasure out
of that lust, those Hindu temple postures and savage bites.
How beautiful, supple we were!

And still, despite crows' feet that give away my age,
I wear cum-fuck-me-shoes. I honour those stabbing luxuries
that once ran down some external obliques, fingers on the run.
Oh, that balcony. A six-pack of love. Just for me, that magic.
Maybe we made tusks. Maybe we made a walrus. Maybe I was a seal.
Don't tell me, still you want me, after all this time.

HOW TO BE A BAD EX-WIFE

Maybe now that our life is spilt, pour a sweet drink on the summer yard. Maybe now that I have raked myself again across every tract of land and through every last room we left empty, we can sip. Now, the ants can come for a sticky bite. Now that I know what I have lost: the maps to the sapphire mine in Montana, the Scotch club files, your preferred drive on forest roads with tamped gravel cliff-views and ditch-sprung waterfalls.

You've taken me for granted. My penance was not eternal. You've taken things we found together, the archaic fish skeletons, the sand dollars, the buffalo bones. I have the lake-white wiccan stones. Maybe now that I miss your quips, your cornflower eyes, your rig-worker thighs. Maybe now I might forgive myself, take my dark insides, give sorrow over to a forgiving sky. Maybe I would stop missing what we should have built, those moors on the shores of the never-never. Now, we can enjoy the light on the water tonight.

DOUBLE FISTING

I'm thinking, on this afternoon of my grand-slam substance abuse, of the children. Two shivering sticks in the autumn lake up to their necks in the current. I've got something in my left hand, something in my right fist. Liquor, drugs, disillusionment. Does it matter what substance I hold tight? This is, after all, the diary of a bad wife throwing it all to the wall, imitating a Greek wedding, an Opa of the heart. Sometimes an ego death needs a little help. It was so easy being not sorry.

BECOME

The crow becomes me in the field
after she takes the songbird's wing,
strips it of feather, meat, explodes bone-feather
to light. There
is a fly's share. There
the ant's feast.

        We try our new sight on the lamp-post.
We preen. We track grey mice,
the prairie vole, the airstream lines,
the black-winged monks' slow gait,
the still tombs, stones, and shopping-cart-
fuss mothers with wriggling babes, their flung-
gummed cookies. Praise the garbage-throwing
teenage boys, their weed-shot eyes and spit cusses
littering the sidewalk's moss!

        I learn the wind through my third
translucent lid, hear the plea of the chickadee.
I know a human squawk, the tug, stretch, tug
of a stubborn gullet-grub, the gleam of a lost dime.

        I move that shiny, river-sparkle to the yard
of my lover: a gift. I hop, one black foot to the other.
I do not see his response to my woman body
cloaked as my feathered self. So, I moult violet
in his sea-eyes, place myself, goddess at the stamen,
and glide into the heady pulse of love.

NO MATTER THE SHAPE OF THINGS, YOU ARE MUCH MISSED

From the room inside, grey mountains
stubborn as a steely cough, a ridged
unrelenting stoop of an unapproving brow.
A dirty look from mother nature.

     The spring heron stands tall on stones,
an early morning dealer of the good stuff,
a bone-soothe from an inside pocket. He's got
a rattle-stop, a throat scuffle cough-drop.

     The sun tips up its brim, eye-bright,
the mountain crests under new light.
Grain spills on the tracks for the spring bear
called The Boss. Magpies glitter over ice,
sky-oil slick as untapped pipelines.

     This stifling monochrome.
I miss bowlegged surety, cornflower and auburn
fields; yesterday morning, certain of its own future.

     In Hindi, there's a legend of a sparrow who erodes
a mountain by dragging a silk scarf across its peak
for one hundred million years. I think of you, us.

     Nothing solid can withstand
that small relentlessness.

INCLEMENT WEATHER

Have you seen the sky turn on a rocky cliff-face,
cobalt silk morph to dappled grey hide,
seen the sky muddle beyond metaphor?
Remember—I loved you. Spectacularly.

From the time I spied you mowing the lawn in your underwear,
to another time, your body slipped in the air, turned and sprung,
off the edge of our vacation boat, back flips for the children,
circus tricks, turns of impatience and longing, while hours
sat across peaceful inhabited rooms, CBC in the speakers droning
the news, almost the same as yesterday, so samey is the turning
of the world, so full of human nature churning. Those days
smutched to years spread soft and grass green.

Let's not forget, none of it was a waste,
let's not forget the mercury moodiness of weather over
the slim, sliced schist jammed sidelong into the continent.
Our marriage was here for the millennia of our lives.
It too has a drift, a motion told in geologic time, a fault line.

I've felt the colour of your mood in my breast.
The ways you despise me now trample down the highway
punch hooves into my chest. But I have not forgotten
your beauty, or the lilies you found at Safeway late on Mothers' Day,
the sun-bleached Celtic glacial tint of your eyes. The talks
we hushed in the bathroom, private and loving, while
our children slept in night-dimmed rooms, hallways away.
Safe then, from me. From us.

There is much to mourn and maybe even much more to say.
But now silence needs a length of time, the forge of memory.

And I have not forgotten the way clouds here scud off
mountain tops and shift a whole sky, the same way tides
scramble oceans. You will never be wrong in our children's DNA.
We will have all of time to sit in those cells patiently together,
all the stories of our past still in synchronicity.

Let those remembrances be balm enough for what has become
of our bombed-out home, empty of my things and the rhythms
we kept. Tell your son, you loved me, keep "once" inside. All
the sky is still in motion. Did you see the weather shift?
Even now, thunderheads might break into blue.

OMEN: CALLA LILIES

and I should have known,

having seen them

in grandma's wedding photo,

the catastrophe of tradition repeating.

I should have known, made another arrangement

for my own bouquet,

when I ordered the water, glass, and paper.

I should have

ordered: Acorns, Arbutus, and Cactus.

Thee only do I love, oh.

*

I should have paid attention to my own singing,
my car-karaoke wisdom.

And if you don't love me now,
You will never love me again ...

And I tried, I took you to the restaurant
with the open-fire kitchen
and the smoking meat.

I sat you at the hot-seat bar and said, I need this, I need this. A list.

No. No. I know I was specific! I'm sure of it. I tried to be a good
communicator.
I said, I need you to love me. And you said, like Popeye,
I yam what I yam.

You said, no.
I asked you to love me and you said,

no.

You didn't say no with one syllable.

You took many more,
pantomimed when necessary,
acted it out, one complacency at a time.

But I couldn't imagine Stevie Nicks fucking Popeye.
So I ordered more champagne.

*

What else could be done?

                    We all get trapped in our own habits,

         don't we?

           My habit was no trap, this time.

                  I watched tiny, glass bubbles float back up to space

        and star-dust.

              None of these details matter.

        Don't we, in our habits, get trapped?

Sometimes such small rearrangements mean all the difference.

                    Or could have.

      The world changed, there at that dinner, the world shifted

      when you said,

          Either you love me or you don't.

And I heard, out loud in my head:

          I guess, I don't.

*

But it all started earlier, in Misty Lake, in July. I asked for it. I looked up
to the sky and said, *make it different*. And I meant it all. Not knowing
how much *all* really meant.

The holidays, their flowered traditions,
and home addresses, home changed too, the habits, the anger,
the washed out, tepid, infrequent love-making, the kitchen knives,
the front yard swing-set,
things I'll never see again.

Because I did not know what this life would ask of me, after that dinner,
because loving me was what you should have wanted.

What you should have been capable of.

Because I did not know

what I could give.
Or take.

*

What happened to the photos I took of the children? Where did you take them?

To your new emptier home? The children, the photo on the bookshelf dusted
with expectations.

My strange, tiny thoughts. All those leftover details.
And me with just my clothes, before you rekeyed all the locks,
so you could help me feel
the thin fabric of sudden exile.

*

And it rippled out from that last October, the man, I think his name was Omen,

    Owen, you corrected me time and again,

        Omen across the street, sold his house and towed his car.

                Remember,

none of these external details matter.

          It isn't who we are.

              But the wild rabbits knew

what Omen meant,

    they ran crazy with change surging in their blood. Bleaching out their own fur

        with the stress of their own thrumming pulse, jacking their feet

under the chilled-day-sky.

             I have shown myself

what I am capable of.

*

Call it the snow globe year.

The year I cracked the big glass ball with all the people inside, all my people,
        even the ones

            we forged out of your sperm and my eggs.

They fell in with all the shards   glass
           and polyester snow-dust.

          Look at the children squiggly, injured,
        amid the dangerous inventory of smashed ideals.

*

I shouldn't have been toying with those wiccan spells
on the sabbats.

All those implications.
All that black magic
in the powerful blood I carry.

Those whispered words were bound for chancy outcomes.

Will your new woman take you out, full moon, full frontal to dance naked
around a fire,
like I did?

What does it matter?
These are just details.

*

I guess you know now I wasn't fucking around

        when I said you needed to protect me from

that guy

        At the party who wanted to take me home,

                while you laughed in the corner.

Remember those old fuse boxes with the switches flipped? Click.

                The sudden dark? Click.

                  No.

        The twisting of the wrong key in the wrong lock? Click.

Say goodbye to the electric panel of my heart.

*

Tonight there was a Coyote in the yard, I wonder,

   was it the first friend you kept in the divorce

     as those old chums divided themselves along his and hers

pack lines?

    Was she creeping by the trembling aspen

  and the wicker chairs?

      Was she listening? Did she hear:

    I slept with another man?

        Did she hear the locksmith pinned me out

bolt by bolt?

My own children would not let me into my left home, were bouncers,

    were party to my lockout.

Did coyote hear the fuse box with her ears pressed to the walls?

    Click,

      Click,

       Click.

   Does it matter?

      Coyote will be the first to tell you,

  you can do better.

I hope you believe her. I hope she's right.

*

But I won't be a standard part replacement,

will I?

No easy cork in the bottle.

And how many times have I replayed the damage

that came out of my mouth?

How many times have you reheard it?

I'm in your head forever.

Know that.

As you are in mine.

I take thee ... in ever-after haunting.

I do.

*

Once, we took the children skiing and handed peanuts to whiskey jacks.

We had such specific luck,

                    but not enough sex to keep us glued.

           Wasn't it enough

                  to keep the best parts of all the other parts?

What the fuck is wrong with me?

                    With you?

*

We are just romantic fools   afoot on stardust

and tapdancing shoes.

Click. Click. Click.

In the room behind the wall, there is a thing that cannot be described by language.

A thing that exists only in the feel of my body.
Is this love, this wakeful trembling, this flood of gratitude,
this canine rage?

I've shown myself
what I'm capable of.

*

I've got such slippery hands.

                            No one should trust me to carry anything,

       really.

Especially,

    people and their blown-glass hearts,

                    in their snow-globe mansions.

*

In the morning, petals blossom out of my eyes and a story falls into daylight.

That time at the Grand Canyon with the children in their raincoats,

and me carrying my anaemia.

That time on the Mt. Stephen scree.

Those midnight feedings.

The scotch-rubbed gums of our daughter. Name things that are pink:

Your knee scar from the car. My untouched nipple.

That damn streetlamp

was such a good companion all those beautiful years.

How I loved you!

Did you hear that?

It was not a waste.

*

May grandmother's silver wedding service blind you
with memories. May you choke on the teacups.

Grandfather's second wife kept all the spoons.   I hope you enjoy
                     all those knives and forks, that wonky setting.

                And my:
My paper art frame, great grandmother's blanket made from her cut up dresses,
my whateverthefuck I can't remember to catalogue for the lawyers, my hand-made
plates, my scent, my favourite mug, a gift from the burlesque troupe, my montana fossils,
        my sense of humour, my white chairs, what does it matter
                  what, my dog, my children, my, my, my
                    nothing a court values.

*

Photos of my children growing up. You claimed them lost
on your rickety hard drive. All.

All the photos of my children growing up are yours
And the aether's.

My children's children's children. Those too are yours.

What will you do with all that stuff, all those trinkets
treasures of my life?
All that dead freight?

*

Came a dream one snowy morning of a tornado cloud, our lake vacation. I've been
here before in this tempest of sky and summer: You are on a dock. The last
chickadee on earth flies out of your mouth. You are that perfect. So
perfect that birds nest in your mouth, and I am a wolf-toothed,
she-beast panting and wild
on the shore, blood-driven and stirred.   .

I shred you,
a whirlwind in a wheat field. All the seeds scatter and bloom tiny
calla lilies
in the sky. I am the
big bad, the big bad,
huffingpuffingthehousedown.

Up-close wind howls at the pasty moon, the star-sprung flowers, NOOOOO, NOOOOOO.

I hear,
Click. Click. Click.
Is it gnashing teeth?
It must be the attic timbers snapping. Those little sticks.
A fuse box of the heart.

Sound weighs nothing in my hands.
Not even weightless
as a glass aorta.

What are you afraid of?
Don't answer that.

*

Just …

Keep it together.

                              Keep it together.

It's all a matter of not knowing, isn't it?
        The strength of a flower is all water and cells.
                        Science doesn't matter when you say:
                        infinitely beautiful.

Romance doesn't need hypothesis and proof.
                        Details don't matter.

I suppose I would have been fine, staying.
                        But
                              that's different from flourishing.

        Keep on keeping on. Keep on swimming. Keep on truckin'.
                        Keep on keeping it together.

        That's the trick, isn't it?
                        Keeping it together.

        I've got such slippery hands.

*

I read a bumper sticker:

Too many freaks, not enough circuses.

I'm always the random freak, circus-less, unexplained.

What did you tell our friends?

Half of them won't talk to me.

What are they afraid of?   That I know what they are?

*

Art is the practice of recognising,

a responsibility to detail.

In the snow globe you were looking at the sky-star-dust. I was looking at the fire.

I was a dwindling ember, and I knew it,

afraid of my own waning glow.

When I left I said,
"for me it's the difference between a good life and an exceptional one."

You said,

"I'm guilty of nothing,

except complacency."

Water seeps out of my cells. Eyes first.

I'm so dehydrated.

I'm bleeding flames.

*

Out out brief candle. Out.
And take all your stuff.

Take your photos, and collections of impressions.
I recall in a dark-hour
in some other decade when my skin is ice-paper and white.

White as calla lily.
Small
as a burst aorta.

*

I am only experimenting with this life I've been given.

The instruction manual

    coded,

        composed of notes I haven't yet glued together.

Directions from the aether, from cells, from dust,

hieroglyphs from space,

    disquieting wisdom from *no place* and *no-one credible.*

*

Instruction manual instructions:

Seventeen pages of metaphor and symbolism from lives I've never led.
                    Something is wrong with my blown-glass monocle.

Name things that can be unmade: a bed, a gift basket ribbon, a marriage.
        Even a batter, once the milk and flour mix, can't be unmade.

                    It's that simple.

*

Beneath the moon. Calla lilies list in the wind, bend, blend to moonlight.

They dream of you.

Like I do.

It's obvious, their faces in my face   in those wedding pictures.

Even then, some miracles couldn't run fast enough

to escape my own mistakes.

And if I sang, I'm sorry.

Would you still dream of me?

Imsorryimsorryimsorryimsorryimsorryimsorryimsorryimsorryimsososorrysorry.

*

Catastrophe recognition: burrows deep in our cells; all the water gathers there,
      seeking its own level.

          Like possibility?

                  Like trust?

It's the kind of day I need a friend.

                It's the kind of day a deer lay supine in the ditch.

The snow-dawn-light gathering   on her bloated flanks and snuffed white corneas.
Her hooves pound the cornflower sky
        in her new right-side-up, up-side-right dream.

*

I should be somewhere else tonight

         handing over my tiny exploded heart
as a hostess gift.

     A bag, like me, of blood, bone, and shards. Here. Have it.

            So nice to see you,
so nice to be here. Such platitudes.

  I wasn't kidding when I told you that you didn't hear me.

            Yes, I did, you said.

*

Instead, I pull a card from the free space at the corner of this game-board:

"The path is long, cold, and wet."

No Kidding, I think aloud into the cornflower clouds.

Little consolation when mortality is an itch in the palm,
a pain in the joints.

A lifetime is beauty, a far-off image,

          some expanse of hazy time,

    butter-whip ground

        and moon-sky-glow.

You promised me things you could not keep.
And I held those against you.

What I am capable of?
I have shown myself.

My skin hurts
from the ice-burn of all that glass-star-dust I've had to pull out of my eyelashes.
After your sales job,
I've got such sore feet from all that dancing.

But,
what a leap!

A ticker-tape of possibility!

*

Still, we are laddered in our children's star-spun DNA.

Look at how beautifully they suffer us,
our foibles.

They are still so very, very sheltered

in my head, in my out loud, in my head,

my knowing.

*

Walk around our old home neighbourhood

take everything you need. Needed.

Still need.

There's no more lock, no more child sentries, no more key.

If you wait, order will tumble itself back into a perfect reality. Remember.

None of these details matter. But they do, don't they?

White petals pour out of our faces.

Our two stardust flowers face up to the cornflower sky.

I trusted you to water me.

But we're made of cosmic-glass-rust.

We've shown each other that much.

*

I was a dark-eyed girl, a dark-eyed beauty,

Huron-French-Celt

       of the misty lake.

              And what were you?

                      A man. A solid man.

What are we capable of? We two?

              Does it matter?

                 This life is all just

     star-dust and vanishing.

And, a calla lily is just a flower   spiral-bloomed hope,

        just a paper wish in the stratosphere,

    or a snow globe

       rolled across the universe,

   just

       glitter, water, glass.

ACKNOWLEDGEMENTS

To my best editors: Each of you have given me something unforgettable and wise through conversation, time, and love. Thank you for the hours of conversation and heart: John Wall Barger, George Elliott Clarke, Bruce Hunter, Patrick Lane, Shelley McAneeley, and Susan Plett. How could I love this crazy, weird poetry life without you?

Special thanks to Anna Weyant. Your paintings smack me in the heart and wake me up. You are singularly astonishing. Keep being amazing, little phenom!

Thanks to Alice Major for her sharp-eyed editing and scouring. This book was in the hands of a master.

Thanks to the staff at the University of Alberta Press.

Special thanks to *Exile* magazine and Michael Callahan for shortlisting portions of the original manuscript for the Gwendolyn MacEwen Poetry Competition.

Special thanks to Caitlyn Voth and Bite Harder Press for choosing "The Crow Takes the Body" for a limited edition broadsheet in 2019. Bless your creative energy. What an amazement.

Thanks, too, for all of you believing and supporting and keeping the enthusiasm alive with talks, interviews, publications, and the joy of creating: Juhyun Tony Bae, Bill Bunn, Marty Gervais, Jeff Kovitz, Dan Lockhart, rob mclennan, Lisa Murphy Lamb, Moira Macdougall, Liz McNally, Natalie Meisner, Susan Musgrave, Richard Osler, Neil Petrunia, Tara Dawn Solheim. Each of you humbles me with your grace and wisdom, and giant capacity to expand poetry's possibility.

An earlier version of "Divorce Sudoku" appeared in *The Literary Review of Canada*, December 2019.

Earlier versions of "(N)ever Thought," "Your Motto," and "She Tells Me" appeared on the Painted Bride Quarterly Podcast #73, "Hornery Is as Hornery Does."

And, of course for contributing various enthusiasms on the way: Ali Bryan, The Electronic Garrett, Aaron Giovannone, Mandy Hagel, Yolanda Hansen, Shaun Hunter, The Kitchen Sink Class (Tyler Engstrom, Josephine LoRe, Ava Maylor, Carley Mayson, Michaela Ritchie, Matt Sutton, Catherine Welburn), Naomi Lewis, Literary Review of Canada, Karen McDonald, Painted Bride Quarterly, Lisa Richter, Bernadette Wagner, Stacey Walyuchow.

Thank you to Ross. It was not a waste and I will believe that until the end of my days.

PROLOGUE: ON OUR FIRST/LAST TOAST

Here's to you, here's to me,
If ever we should disagree,
Fuck you, and here's to me.

EPILOGUE

Out beyond ideas of wrongdoing and rightdoing,
is a field. I'll meet you there.
—Rumi

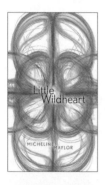

Little Wildheart

MICHELINE MAYLOR

Quirky, startling, earthy poems reflect the moods of existence.

Robert Kroetsch Series

Deriving

JENNIFER BOWERING DELISLE

Deriving explores infertility, motherhood, and family, while troubling colonial legacies of language and Canadian identity.

Robert Kroetsch Series

To float, to drown, to close up, to open

E. ALEX PIERCE

Accomplished poet's new collection of sensuous, intelligent poems that contemplate art, memory, and personal longing.

Robert Kroetsch Series

More information at uap.ualberta.ca